I0695747

Crafting Blockbusters

AI Dissects the Top 5 Bestselling Classics

A Little Tree Food Forest Publication

ISBN 9798859204656

Table of Contents

Chapter 1
Don Quixote
Tilting at Windmills and Literary Adventures

Ah, Don Quixote! The knight whose armor was a touch rusty and whose sanity might have been a bit wobbly, but whose spirit was as valiant as any in the realm of literature. If ever there was a character who embodied the phrase "tilting at windmills," it was our dear, deluded Don. But oh, what an adventure he took us on! So, my fellow literary explorers, fasten your helmets and saddle up as we embark on a journey through the pages of Cervantes' masterwork and dive headfirst into the windmills of imagination, the quirks of characters, and the layers of narrative brilliance.

A Knightly Start - Deconstructing the Opening

"Somewhere in La Mancha, in a place whose name I do not care to remember, a gentleman lived not long ago, one of those who has a lance and ancient shield on a shelf and keeps a skinny nag and a greyhound for racing." Ah, what a way to kick off an adventure! Cervantes knew how to grab our attention right from the start. This opening line is like a warm-up for a grand performance, a nod to the readers that they're about to witness something extraordinary, or perhaps gloriously absurd.

Don Quixote, or Alonso Quixano as he's known before his knightly rebranding, sets off with his trusty sidekick Sancho Panza on a quest that turns reality into a playground of chivalry, giants, and, of course, those infamous windmills. Cervantes serves us the perfect blend of humor and depth in this opening, hinting at the whimsical and poignant tale that's about to unfold.

Windmills of Imagination
Delving into Setting and World-Building

Step into the world of Don Quixote, where the landscapes are as much a character as the protagonist himself. La Mancha, with its sprawling plains and dusty roads, serves as a canvas for Quixote's wandering mind. Every inn becomes a castle, and every passerby a potential adversary. Cervantes masterfully blurs the lines between reality and illusion, creating a stage where our hero's imagination can run wild.

And those windmills! Oh, those windmills. They stand tall and majestic, yet, in Quixote's eyes, they morph into menacing giants, waiting to be battled. This transformation is a brilliant testament to the power of perception. Cervantes invites us to question what we see and to consider how our own lenses shape the world around us. The windmills become symbols of the challenges we face and the courage it takes to confront them, no matter how quixotic the endeavor.

Quirks and Quests - Unraveling the Characters

Let's talk characters, shall we? Starting with our protagonist, Don Quixote himself. He's a concoction of idealism, delusion, and an insatiable appetite for the chivalrous. Quixote embodies the spirit of adventure, reminding us that even in our ordinary lives, there's room for quests and grandeur. His transformation from a gentleman with dusty tomes to a knight with dusty armor is a reminder that it's never too late to chase your dreams, even if they involve jousting with windmills.

Sancho Panza, the faithful squire, is the grounding force in this whirlwind of delusions. With a penchant for proverbs and a practical outlook on life, Sancho provides the perfect counterbalance to Quixote's lofty ideals. He's the voice of reason, the sidekick we all need when our aspirations threaten to float too far into the ether.

Act by Act - Plotting the Playful Escapades

Cervantes' plot dances between farce and philosophy, meandering through encounters that test both the characters and the readers. We witness Quixote's encounters with perplexed locals, outraged priests, and scorned lovers. Each escapade serves as a satirical mirror to human nature, reflecting our own tendency to wrestle with reality and illusion.

But let's not forget the heart of the story—the quest for Dulcinea, a lady so virtuous that her existence becomes both a motivating force and an unattainable ideal. Quixote's unwavering dedication to Dulcinea speaks to the power of faith and how it can shape our perception of reality.

Pen Mightier Than the Sword
Exploring Writing Styles

Cervantes' writing style is a character in its own right, effortlessly shifting from comedic to introspective, from playful banter to profound musings. The narrative takes on various forms, including epistolary exchanges and tales within tales. This stylistic versatility keeps us engaged, inviting us to view the story through different lenses and appreciate the multifaceted nature of storytelling.

Cervantes' language, though rooted in the 17th century, feels remarkably modern in its humor and accessibility. He invites us into the world of Don Quixote with open arms, making even the most archaic expressions relatable and entertaining. It's as if Cervantes is winking at us across the centuries, saying, "This tale is timeless, and you're in on the joke."

The Meta Twist - Cervantes' Narrative Devices

And now, for the pièce de résistance—the meta twist. Cervantes takes us further down the rabbit hole by presenting Don Quixote as a manuscript within the novel itself. Characters within the story read about Quixote's adventures, blurring the boundaries between creator and creation, reader and character.

This narrative device adds layers of complexity to the story's exploration of reality and fiction. It's a nod to the power of storytelling to shape our perception of the world, both within the pages and beyond. Cervantes challenges us to consider the ways in which stories influence our own lives, just as Quixote's tales shape the lives of those he encounters.

In Conclusion

Don Quixote isn't just a novel; it's a literary adventure that takes us on a journey through the realms of imagination, perception, and the very nature of storytelling. Cervantes' wit, wisdom, and narrative genius have left an indelible mark on the literary landscape. As we close the first chapter of our analysis, let's raise a proverbial lance to Don Quixote, that gallant knight who taught us to see giants where windmills stand and to dream impossible dreams. Onward, dear reader, to the windmills of the next chapter!

Chapter 2
A Tale of Two Cities
Revolutionary Prose and Parallel Plots

Ladies and gentlemen, brace yourselves for a literary journey that traverses not only two cities but also the tumultuous landscape of the human spirit. In Charles Dickens' "A Tale of Two Cities," we're thrown headfirst into the turmoil of the French Revolution, and trust me, this isn't your average history lesson. So, tighten your cravats and don your bonnets as we delve into the opening lines, the dual identities of cities, the dramatic interplay of characters, and the revolutionary brilliance of Dickens' narrative craftsmanship.

Opening Lines and Historical Insights

"It was the best of times, it was the worst of times..." If there ever was an opening line that managed to capture the essence of an entire epoch, this is it. Dickens doesn't tiptoe around; he plunges us straight into the turbulent waters of the French Revolution with a philosophical precision that'd make a philosopher jealous. The duality of those lines isn't just a stylistic flourish; it's a thematic declaration that sets the stage for the dualities to come.

And speaking of setting the stage, Dickens is renowned for his knack for depicting historical backdrops with exquisite detail. The foggy streets of London, imbued with an air of nostalgia, stand in stark contrast to the revolutionary fervor of Paris. Dickens isn't just giving us a glimpse of two cities; he's painting a portrait of an era, and it's as vivid as a Turner painting.

Cities as Characters - London and Paris Speak

Hold on, did someone say cities as characters? Oh, yes, indeed. In Dickens' world, London and Paris aren't mere settings; they're living, breathing entities. London is the city of contrasts, a place where wealth and squalor rub shoulders, where dandyism and destitution coexist. It's like a patchwork quilt stitched together with the threads of class disparity.

And then there's Paris, a city teetering on the precipice of revolution. Dickens captures the chaos and hope that permeate the atmosphere, painting a cityscape that mirrors the struggles and aspirations of its inhabitants. From the wine-stained streets to the shadow of the guillotine, Paris becomes more than a backdrop; it's a character entwined with the destinies of its people.

Double the Drama
Analyzing Characters in Contrasts

Let's talk characters, shall we? Dickens has a knack for creating characters that feel like they're pulled straight from the tapestry of life. We have Charles Darnay and Sydney Carton, two men who are polar opposites and yet bound by a peculiar fate. Darnay is the aristocratic figure who rejects his family's privilege, while Carton is the disillusioned cynic with a hidden depth of selflessness.

And then there's the enigmatic Lucie Manette, a symbol of light and hope in a world of darkness. Lucie, embodying purity and compassion, has the ability to bring out the best in those around her. Even her father, Dr. Manette, emerges from the shadows of his traumatic past to find solace in her presence. These characters are more than pawns on a literary chessboard; they're reflections of the human condition.

Threads Intertwined
Unveiling the Dual Plot Structure

Now, brace yourself for some literary magic. Dickens doesn't just give us one plot; he hands us two, intricately woven together like a beautifully complex tapestry. The personal drama of the characters intersects seamlessly with the historical turmoil of the French Revolution. It's as if Dickens is saying, "Hey, the revolution isn't just about mobs and guillotines; it's about the lives it touches."

The way Dickens intertwines the personal and the political is a masterstroke of storytelling. Every twist and turn in the characters' lives resonates with the broader sociopolitical landscape, creating a sense of inevitability and fate. Whether it's the courtroom drama of Darnay or the redemption arc of Carton, their journeys are inseparable from the upheaval of the times.

The Guillotine's Pen
Writing the Pinnacle of Tension

If you thought Dickens was content with weaving intricate characters and settings, think again. He cranks up the tension like a master composer building to a crescendo. The climax of "A Tale of Two Cities" isn't just a dramatic courtroom scene or a love confession; it's the looming shadow of the guillotine. The blade of destiny hangs over the characters' heads, and Dickens keeps us teetering on the edge.

The build-up to the ultimate sacrifice is a study in tension. Carton's selfless act, with its echoes of resurrection and sacrifice, is a culmination of his character arc and the broader themes of the novel. Dickens uses the guillotine not just as a tool of execution, but as a symbol of the sweeping change that revolution brings—a change that can both unite and divide.

Dickensian Flourishes
Language that Leaves a Mark

Ah, the language of Dickens! It's like a feast for the senses, an explosion of adjectives and imagery that transports us to another time. His descriptions are vivid and poetic, his dialogue a symphony of distinct voices. From the crunch of carriage wheels on cobblestones to the cacophony of a Parisian street, Dickens' prose makes us feel like we're walking alongside the characters.

And let's not forget his wry humor and biting social commentary. Dickens infuses the narrative with his signature wit, using satire to expose the absurdities of both aristocracy and revolution. His characters' idiosyncrasies are a source of both amusement and introspection, a reminder that even in the darkest of times, human nature retains its quirks.

In Conclusion

And there you have it—a tale of revolution, redemption, and resurrection. Dickens' "A Tale of Two Cities" isn't just a historical novel; it's a tapestry of human experience, woven with threads of sacrifice, love, and the indomitable human spirit. So, my fellow readers, as we bid adieu to the double-edged drama of London and Paris, let's carry with us the echoes of Dickens' prose and the resounding message that, indeed, it was the best of times, it was the worst of times. Onward, to the next chapter of literary exploration!

Chapter 3
The Lord of the Rings
Ringing Fantasies and Epic World-Building

Gather 'round, my fellow adventurers, for we're about to embark on a journey of epic proportions through the hallowed pages of J.R.R. Tolkien's "The Lord of the Rings." Elves, dwarves, hobbits, and a certain jewelry problem await us. So, fasten your elven cloaks and ready your walking sticks, as we delve into the cozy beginnings, the vast realms of Middle-earth, the fellowship of unlikely heroes, and the linguistic symphony that Tolkien orchestrated.

A Shire Beginning - The Art of the Inviting Start

"In a hole in the ground, there lived a hobbit." With those ten words, Tolkien ensnares us in the charm of the Shire, a world of comfort and coziness that quickly becomes our second home. The opening lines are a testament to the power of simplicity; they invite us into a world of relatable simplicity before sweeping us away into grand adventures.

Tolkien's gentle pacing and whimsical descriptions set the tone for the journey ahead. We meet Bilbo Baggins, the quintessential hobbit, and follow him as he's whisked away on an unexpected adventure. The Shire's tranquility becomes a backdrop against which the epic quest unfolds, making it all the more impactful when the world expands beyond its borders.

Middle-earth Unveiled
Crafting a World with Depth

Ah, Middle-earth — a realm as vast and varied as a wizard's wardrobe. Tolkien's world-building is nothing short of legendary, a masterclass in creating a universe that feels both ancient and alive. From the rolling hills of the Shire to the shadowy depths of Mordor, every corner of Middle-earth is meticulously crafted, each with its own history, cultures, and languages.

Tolkien's attention to detail extends to flora, fauna, and even the constellations that dot the night sky. He's not just an author; he's an architect, constructing a universe with layers of depth that beckon readers to lose themselves in its intricacies. Whether it's the grand cities of Gondor or the humble homes of the hobbits, Middle-earth isn't just a setting — it's a character in its own right.

Fellowship of Characters
Strengths in Diversity

Hold onto your wizard's hat, because here come the characters. Frodo, Sam, Aragorn, Gandalf, Legolas, Gimli, Boromir, Merry, and Pippin — they're not just characters; they're comrades in arms, bound by a common purpose and the bonds of friendship. Tolkien's fellowship is a microcosm of the world he's built, a mosaic of races and personalities that reflect the diversity of Middle-earth.

Each character brings their own strengths and vulnerabilities to the table. Frodo's quiet determination, Sam's unwavering loyalty, and Aragorn's regal leadership — they're not just protagonists; they're reflections of virtues we aspire to possess. And through their interactions, Tolkien showcases the power of unity, reminding us that even in the face of darkness, the light of friendship can guide us.

**Journey Unbound
Tracing the Multi-layered Plot**

Let's talk plot. "The Lord of the Rings" isn't just a quest to destroy a certain pesky ring; it's a symphony of subplots, alliances, and betrayals that crescendo toward a climactic showdown. The journey isn't just physical; it's emotional and moral, a reflection of the characters' growth and the challenges they overcome.

Tolkien takes us on a rollercoaster through territories both familiar and treacherous. From the Mines of Moria to the Plains of Rohan, the narrative paints landscapes that mirror the characters' internal struggles. Frodo's battle against the lure of the ring and Aragorn's journey from ranger to king are woven together with the broader narrative, creating a tapestry of personal and collective transformation.

**Climactic Showdowns
Forging Moments of Ultimate Peril**

Hold onto your elven cloaks, for the climactic showdowns are upon us. Tolkien's ability to ratchet up tension and suspense is akin to Gandalf summoning fireworks on Hobbiton's Green Dragon Inn. Whether it's the chase through the Mines of Moria or the Battle of Helm's Deep, the stakes keep escalating, leaving us breathless with anticipation.

And let's not forget the ultimate confrontation at Mount Doom. Frodo's struggle against the weight of the One Ring is a battle of willpower and determination, a testament to the human spirit's capacity to overcome even the most insurmountable odds. Tolkien's mastery lies in his ability to create moments that are not just epic in scale, but also deeply personal.

Tolkien's Linguistic Mastery
Language as a Cultural Artifact

Prepare to be amazed, for Tolkien wasn't just content with building a world; he constructed languages to go along with it. Elvish, Dwarvish, and even Black Speech—they're not just linguistic curiosities; they're integral to the fabric of Middle-earth's cultures. The languages aren't mere decorations; they're windows into the hearts and minds of the races that speak them.

Tolkien's linguistic brilliance isn't just about inventing new words; it's about capturing the essence of cultures and civilizations. Elvish flows like a melody, while Dwarvish is as robust as the people who forged it. And the languages' evolution over time mirrors the rise and fall of empires, making them cultural artifacts that enrich the tapestry of Middle-earth.

In Conclusion

And there you have it, my fellow travelers—an exploration of Tolkien's "The Lord of the Rings." From the humble beginnings of the Shire to the heart-pounding battles of Mordor, we've journeyed through a world both fantastical and familiar. So, as we conclude this chapter of our literary escapade, let's raise a glass (or an elven goblet) to Middle-earth, a realm that reminds us that even in the darkest of times, courage and friendship can light the way. Onward, to the next chapter of adventure!

Chapter 4
The Little Prince
Whimsical Wisdom and Allegorical Charm

Ladies and gentlemen, gather around, for we're about to embark on a journey to a world where roses talk, foxes impart wisdom, and planets hold profound meaning. Antoine de Saint-Exupéry's "The Little Prince" isn't just a children's tale; it's a masterpiece that enchants both young and old with its whimsical wisdom and allegorical charm. So, put on your aviator's goggles and prepare for liftoff as we delve into the timelessness of its opening, the layers of symbolism, the royal friendships that shape its narrative, and the allegorical delights that await.

Once Upon a Timelessness
Capturing Time in the Opening

"In the book of the records of my memory..." With these opening words, Saint-Exupéry invites us to travel through time itself. The Little Prince's story is woven into the fabric of memory, reminding us that tales are as ancient as the stars and as enduring as the winds. The opening is like an old leather-bound book, weathered by time and waiting to share its wisdom.

Saint-Exupéry's language evokes a sense of nostalgia and wonder, setting the stage for a story that transcends the boundaries of age and generation. It's as if he's whispering, "Come, dear reader, let me take you on a journey that stretches across the sands of time."

Planets of Meaning
Decoding Symbolism and Themes

Ah, the planets—the celestial playground where the Little Prince encounters a cast of characters that are as diverse as they are symbolic. The lamplighter, the geographer, the king—they're not just whimsical figures; they're reflections of human nature and society. Saint-Exupéry uses them to mirror the idiosyncrasies and absurdities of the adult world.

But let's not forget the asteroid B-612 and its single rose. The rose, with its vanity and vulnerability, becomes a metaphor for love, friendship, and the complexities of human relationships. Saint-Exupéry takes us beyond the literal, inviting us to explore the layers of meaning that lie beneath the surface.

Royalty in Friendships
Characters as Reflections

Now, let's talk about friendships that bloom in the desert of loneliness. The fox—the wise, enigmatic creature—teaches the Little Prince that taming isn't about control; it's about connection. Their bond becomes an allegory for the power of relationships, the beauty of vulnerability, and the significance of genuine connection.

And then there's the Little Prince's royal lineage, which isn't about crowns and castles but about understanding and empathy. His friendship with the narrator, the Aviator, becomes a reflection of the genuine connections that can bridge the gap between generations and cultures. Through these friendships, Saint-Exupéry teaches us that true royalty lies not in titles, but in the authenticity of our hearts.

Short, Sweet, and Significant
Crafting a Compact Plot

Let's take a moment to appreciate the elegance of Saint-Exupéry's storytelling. "The Little Prince" isn't a sprawling epic; it's a compact masterpiece that distills profound truths into a concise narrative. Every word carries weight, every encounter is rich with meaning, and every moment is a gem waiting to be uncovered.

The story's brevity is its strength; it's a lesson in saying more with less. Saint-Exupéry invites us to embrace the power of simplicity, reminding us that even in a world of noise, the whispers of wisdom can still be heard.

Art of Innocence
Balancing Depth with Simplicity

"Sometimes, there is no harm in putting off a piece of work until another day." This simple statement from the fox encapsulates the beauty of innocence and the depth of its wisdom. Saint-Exupéry's tale dances between childlike wonder and profound truths, reminding us that the most complex ideas can be expressed through the simplicity of a child's perspective.

The innocence of the Little Prince is a mirror that reflects the purity of childhood imagination and the naiveté that can lead to the discovery of life's deepest truths. Saint-Exupéry invites us to embrace that innocence, to view the world through unfiltered lenses, and to find wonder in the most ordinary of things.

Reading Between the Lines
Allegory and its Delights

And now, my dear readers, let's dive into the heart of "The Little Prince"—its allegorical brilliance. Saint-Exupéry doesn't just tell a story; he crafts an allegory that's both universal and deeply personal. The Little Prince's travels become a mirror that reflects our own journey through life — the discoveries, the disappointments, and the relationships that shape us.

But allegory isn't just about finding meaning; it's about the delight of discovery. Every encounter, every conversation with a rose or a fox, becomes a puzzle piece that fits into the larger picture of human existence. Saint-Exupéry challenges us to read between the lines, to unearth the hidden truths, and to find delight in the process of interpretation.

In Conclusion

And there you have it, my fellow travelers — a whimsical journey through the allegorical wonderland of "The Little Prince." From planets that speak volumes to friendships that transcend time, Saint-Exupéry's tale is a masterpiece that captures the essence of human nature in a deceptively simple narrative. So, as we bid adieu to the Little Prince and his cosmic adventures, let's carry with us the lessons of friendship, innocence, and the timeless wisdom that dwells within the pages of this charming fable. Onward, to the next chapter of enchantment!

Chapter 5
Harry Potter and the Philosopher's Stone
Enchantment and Coming-of-Age

Greetings, fellow wizards and witches! Ready your wands and dust off your broomsticks, for we're about to dive into the enchanting world of J.K. Rowling's "Harry Potter and the Philosopher's Stone." This isn't just a story about a boy and his magical destiny; it's a tale of wonder, friendship, and the trials of growing up in a world where spells are as common as textbooks. So, don your invisibility cloak and prepare for a journey through the wizarding welcomes, the magical realm of Hogwarts, the diverse array of characters, the mysteries that unfold, and the spellbinding magic that lies within the ordinary.

Wizarding Welcomes
The Portal to Rowling's World

"Mr. and Mrs. Dursley of number four, Privet Drive, were proud to say that they were perfectly normal, thank you very much." And thus begins a tale that would redefine the concept of normalcy. Rowling's opening lines are like a gateway to a world where letters fly, owls deliver news, and a boy's destiny is marked by a lightning-shaped scar.

Rowling's wizarding world isn't just a setting; it's an invitation to leave the mundane behind and embrace the extraordinary. With a dash of humor and a sprinkle of whimsy, Rowling transports us to a realm where magical creatures roam, spells are cast, and the pages are alive with the promise of enchantment.

Hogwarts and Beyond
Building a Magical Reality

Ah, Hogwarts School of Witchcraft and Wizardry — every child's dream and every adult's yearning for a second chance at education. Rowling's creation of Hogwarts isn't just about ivy-covered walls and moving staircases; it's about the sense of belonging and the discovery of self that education can bring.

Rowling's meticulous world-building extends beyond the school's walls. Diagon Alley, with its quirky shops and bustling atmosphere, becomes a microcosm of the wizarding world's diversity and eccentricities. From Gringotts to Ollivanders, each corner is a testament to the layers of depth that Rowling injects into her universe.

Characters in Every House
Lessons in Diversity

Let's talk about the characters that bring Hogwarts to life. Harry, Hermione, Ron, and the rest of the gang aren't just protagonists; they're reflections of the human experience. Harry's longing for family, Hermione's thirst for knowledge, Ron's loyalty — they're traits that resonate with readers of all ages.

And let's not forget the diversity within the Hogwarts houses. Gryffindor, Slytherin, Hufflepuff, and Ravenclaw aren't just dormitories; they're allegories for the multifaceted nature of human personalities. Rowling teaches us that it's not about which house you're sorted into; it's about the choices you make and the friendships you cultivate.

Mysteries Unveiled
Untangling the Threads of the Plot

The Philosopher's Stone isn't just a magical rock; it's the crux of a mystery that keeps us flipping pages faster than a Quidditch snitch. Rowling's plot isn't just a series of events; it's a tapestry of clues, twists, and revelations that engage both the intellect and the heart.

As Harry, Ron, and Hermione investigate the stone's whereabouts, they encounter challenges that test their courage, intelligence, and loyalty. Rowling's storytelling is a delicate balance of tension and warmth, keeping us on the edge of our seats while simultaneously inviting us to revel in the camaraderie of the trio's friendship.

Dueling Fates
Climax and Confrontation

Ah, the climax—the point in every great story where the stakes reach their peak. Rowling's portrayal of the confrontation in the bowels of Hogwarts is a symphony of tension and emotion. The showdown with Voldemort, the ultimate dark wizard, is not just a battle of spells; it's a battle of wills, a clash of destinies.

But it's not just about flashy wand-waving. Rowling infuses the climax with moments of sacrifice, bravery, and love. From Dumbledore's wisdom to Harry's motherly protection, the climax is a culmination of themes that echo throughout the narrative—the triumph of good over evil, the power of love, and the resilience of the human spirit.

Magic in the Mundane
Making the Extraordinary Ordinary

And now, let's talk about the magic that's woven into the fabric of everyday life. Rowling's genius lies in her ability to find enchantment in the mundane. From the charms that clean dishes to the pensieve that stores memories, magic becomes an extension of reality rather than an escape from it.

Rowling teaches us that magic isn't just about waving wands; it's about the choices we make and the impact we have on the world around us. The Philosopher's Stone, with its promise of eternal life, becomes a mirror that reflects our own desires and the importance of embracing the present moment.

In Conclusion

And there you have it, my fellow spellbinders — an exploration of "Harry Potter and the Philosopher's Stone." From the humble beginnings on Privet Drive to the climactic showdown at Hogwarts, Rowling's tale is a journey of discovery, friendship, and the magic that lies within us all. So, as we bid adieu to our wizarding adventure, let's carry with us the lessons of courage, loyalty, and the understanding that even in a world of magic, it's the human connections that truly matter. Onward, to the next chapter of enchantment!

Chapter 6
Threads That Bind
Common Themes Among Bestsellers

Ladies, gentlemen, and literary enthusiasts of all ages, welcome to the heart of our analysis — a chapter that weaves together the golden threads that unite the bestselling novels we've explored. Whether you've tilted at windmills, traversed two cities, journeyed through Middle-earth, flown with the Little Prince, or cast spells at Hogwarts, you've undoubtedly noticed that beneath the surface, these tales share common themes that resonate across time and culture. So, grab your quills and parchments as we delve into the transformative quests, evolving characters, immersive worlds, climactic showdowns, and narrative techniques that thread their way through these stories like the spine of a well-loved book.

Quests and Journeys
Embarking on Transformative Adventures

What's an epic tale without a quest? From Don Quixote's chivalrous escapades to Harry Potter's magical battles, our protagonists are often thrown into adventures that challenge their status quo. These quests aren't just about physical journeys; they're about internal transformations, the metamorphosis of characters from who they are to who they must become.

Each quest becomes a crucible where characters confront their fears, question their beliefs, and discover their strengths. Whether it's Harry facing his own destiny or Frodo wrestling with the weight of the One Ring, the journey isn't just about reaching a destination; it's about becoming the hero of one's own story.

Characters in Growth
The Evolution of Protagonists

Let's talk about character arcs, shall we? One of the universal truths of storytelling is that characters evolve. Don Quixote sheds his delusions and gains self-awareness, Sydney Carton finds redemption in "A Tale of Two Cities," and the Little Prince learns the importance of connection. These characters aren't just ink on paper; they're mirrors that reflect the human experience.

Their growth isn't linear; it's a dance of setbacks and triumphs. It's Hermione learning to embrace her intelligence, Aragorn stepping into his destiny, and Harry navigating the complexities of adolescence while fighting dark forces. Characters that change and adapt are characters that feel real, and their evolution resonates with readers because it mirrors our own journeys of self-discovery.

World-Building Wonders
Crafting Immersive Settings

Ah, world-building—the art of creating places that feel as real as your favorite coffee shop. Whether it's the fantastical landscapes of Middle-earth or the enchanting corridors of Hogwarts, the settings in these novels aren't just backdrops; they're living, breathing entities that shape the narrative.

The attention to detail in each world is what makes them come alive. The streets of Paris in "A Tale of Two Cities" feel as tangible as the cobblestones beneath your feet, and the magical creatures in "Harry Potter" inhabit the realm of the believable. These settings aren't just windows; they're doorways that invite readers to step into a new reality.

Climactic Showdowns
Pinnacles of Tension and Release

Picture this: the tension is palpable, the stakes are sky-high, and the fate of characters hangs in the balance. Ah, the climactic showdown—a moment that's as satisfying as a final puzzle piece snapping into place. Whether it's Harry facing off against Voldemort or Frodo standing before Mount Doom, these showdowns are the crescendos that bring the narrative to its zenith.

But it's not just about flashy action scenes; it's about emotional investment. Will the hero succeed? Will the villain be vanquished? These showdowns become a microcosm of the broader themes—the triumph of good over evil, the resilience of the human spirit, and the power of unity.

Narrative Techniques
Tools of Masterful Storytelling

Now, let's dive into the craft of storytelling itself. Whether it's Cervantes, Dickens, Tolkien, Saint-Exupéry, or Rowling, these authors wield a toolbox filled with narrative techniques that elevate their tales. They manipulate perspectives, employ foreshadowing, and use symbolism to layer their stories with depth and meaning.

Cervantes' meta twist, Dickens' vivid prose, Tolkien's linguistic mastery, Saint-Exupéry's allegorical brilliance, and Rowling's enchanting realism—all these techniques serve as instruments in a symphony of storytelling. Whether it's a sentence that captures the essence of an era or a chapter that keeps us turning pages, these authors show us that the art of writing is as diverse and rich as the stories themselves.

In Conclusion

And there you have it, my fellow readers—a tapestry woven from the common threads that bind these bestselling novels. From quests that transform to characters that grow, from immersive worlds to climactic showdowns, and from narrative techniques that dazzle to themes that resonate, these elements come together to create stories that endure the test of time.

So, as we close this chapter of exploration, let's carry with us the understanding that great literature isn't just about individual novels; it's about the collective wisdom, human experiences, and shared truths that span the breadth of human imagination. Onward, to the final chapter where we distill these insights into writing tips that will ignite your own literary endeavors!

Chapter 7
Style Palette
Exploring Narrative Techniques

Greetings, dear writers and word enthusiasts! We've ventured through the whimsy of "Don Quixote," the revolutions of "A Tale of Two Cities," the realms of Middle-earth, the stars with the Little Prince, and the enchanted corridors of Hogwarts. Now, we're donning our writerly hats to explore the artistry behind these tales—the narrative techniques that shape their unique voices, keeping us spellbound from the first line to the last. From finding the right tone to playing with time, let's dive into the writer's style palette with the enthusiasm of a wizard discovering a new spell.

Voice Matters - Finding the Right Tone and Style

Picture this: Don Quixote's gallant declarations, the solemnity of "A Tale of Two Cities," the lyrical cadence of Tolkien, the allegorical charm of the Little Prince, and the enchanting realism of Rowling. Each author crafts a distinct voice that becomes the lens through which we experience their worlds.

Voice isn't just about the words on the page; it's about the emotional connection they create. Cervantes' whimsical tone engages us in Don Quixote's fantastical delusions, while Dickens' somber style immerses us in the turmoil of revolution. As writers, we must find the voice that suits our story's heart—the one that resonates with readers, evoking laughter, tears, or a sense of wonder.

Pacing and Suspense
Keeping Readers on the Edge

Ah, pacing—the heartbeat of a narrative. Whether it's the relentless action of "The Lord of the Rings" or the slow build of tension in "Harry Potter," pacing is the secret ingredient that keeps readers glued to the pages. It's the art of knowing when to speed up the tempo and when to linger in the moment.

Suspense, on the other hand, is the promise of something thrilling around the corner. Tolkien's cliffhangers, Saint-Exupéry's allegorical hints, and Rowling's mysteries—they all keep us guessing, turning pages to uncover the secrets hidden in the shadows. Balancing pacing and suspense is like conducting an orchestra; it's about the ebb and flow that keeps readers invested.

Dialogue Dynamics
The Art of Natural Conversations

Ever eavesdrop on a conversation that's so riveting, you forget you're not part of it? That's the magic of well-crafted dialogue. From Sancho Panza's banter with Don Quixote to the philosophical exchanges in "The Little Prince," dialogue is a vehicle for character development and narrative propulsion.

Good dialogue isn't just about realism; it's about efficiency. Every word should count, revealing something about the characters or moving the plot forward. It's the rhythm of back-and-forth, the unspoken emotions, and the subtext that keeps us engaged. As writers, our dialogue is a symphony of voices—distinct, dynamic, and a reflection of the human experience.

Flashbacks and Foreshadowing
Playing with Time

Ah, time—the canvas on which stories are painted. Flashbacks and foreshadowing are the artist's tools, allowing us to manipulate time like a magician. Dickens' weaving of past and present in "A Tale of Two Cities," Tolkien's ancient histories in "The Lord of the Rings," and Rowling's enigmatic prophecies—they all add layers of depth to their narratives.

Flashbacks give context, revealing the layers beneath a character's façade. Foreshadowing, on the other hand, is like breadcrumbs leading to a grand revelation. It's the art of hinting at what's to come without giving away the entire plot. These techniques are time-travel for writers, allowing us to create intricate narratives that unfold like puzzles.

The Art of Show and Tell - Evoking Imagination

We've all heard the maxim "Show, don't tell," but what does it really mean? It's about evoking imagery that dances in the reader's mind. Cervantes' vivid descriptions, Tolkien's landscapes that beg to be explored, Saint-Exupéry's allegorical vignettes—they all invite readers to step into their worlds.

"Show, don't tell" isn't a prohibition on telling; it's a call to create experiences. It's about letting readers feel the chill in the air, taste the dust of the road, and smell the parchment in the library. It's the difference between reading and experiencing. As writers, our words are brushes, and our readers' minds are canvases waiting to be painted.

In Conclusion

And there you have it, my fellow wordsmiths—a journey through the writer's style palette. From finding the right voice to mastering pacing, from crafting authentic dialogue to playing with time, and from the art of showing to the thrill of foreshadowing, these techniques are the colors that fill the canvas of storytelling.

So, as we conclude this chapter, let's carry with us the understanding that style isn't just about pretty prose; it's about the tools that bring stories to life. Like painters with palettes and musicians with instruments, writers wield these techniques to create worlds that captivate, characters that resonate, and narratives that linger long after the final page is turned. Onward, to the grand finale—where we distill these insights into writing tips that will inspire your own literary endeavors!

Chapter 8
Beyond the Words
Visualizing Scenes and Settings

Greetings, fellow architects of words! In our grand exploration of the art of storytelling, we've tilted at windmills, traversed cities, journeyed through magical realms, soared with the Little Prince, and cast spells at Hogwarts. Now, it's time to step beyond the confines of letters and punctuation, delving into a realm where words become images, and scenes and settings are painted with the vivid strokes of imagination. So, grab your mental sketch pads and let's explore the craft of visualizing scenes and settings—a skill that turns words into cinematic experiences.

Cinematic Vision
Painting Scenes with Vivid Imagery

Imagine reading a description that's so vivid, it feels like a movie playing in your mind. That's the magic of cinematic vision. Authors like Cervantes, Dickens, Tolkien, Saint-Exupéry, and Rowling are masters at creating images that spring to life. They don't just tell us what's happening; they show us the scene, inviting us to be spectators in our own imaginations.

Cinematic vision is about invoking imagery that's both specific and evocative. Instead of saying "It was a sunny day," authors use metaphors, similes, and precise details to immerse us in the scene. The sunlight becomes "a golden curtain that swept away the shadows," turning a simple description into a multi sensory experience.

Sensory Symphony - Engaging All the Senses

Close your eyes and imagine stepping into a bustling marketplace. Can you hear the chatter, smell the spices, and feel the energy? That's the magic of sensory engagement. When authors invoke the senses, they create scenes that are immersive and unforgettable.

Dickens' descriptions of the streets in "A Tale of Two Cities" transport us to the gritty alleys of Paris, the smell of horses mingling with the scent of desperation. Rowling's feasts at Hogwarts make our mouths water, and Tolkien's descriptions of the Shire evoke the feeling of fresh grass underfoot. Engaging the senses isn't just about seeing; it's about tasting, touching, smelling, and hearing the world the characters inhabit.

Set Dressing - Using Settings to Enhance Mood

Settings aren't just backdrops; they're integral to the mood of a scene. Whether it's the foreboding atmosphere of a dungeon or the enchantment of a castle, settings can be as influential as characters. Authors are like set designers, using descriptions to create the stage on which their narratives unfold.

The spooky vibe of Don Quixote's encounters in windmills is set by the desolate landscape and eerie wind. Rowling's Forbidden Forest is filled with allure and danger of the unknown. As writers, our settings aren't just physical; they're emotional. We use them to convey the tone, mirror the characters' states of mind, and heighten tension or tranquility.

Dynamic Descriptions
Balancing Detail and Brevity

Ah, the art of description—the tightrope walk between lavish detail and succinct brevity. Too much detail, and readers might get lost in the minutiae; too little, and the scene feels hollow. Finding the balance is the key to dynamic descriptions.

Cervantes' elaborate descriptions of Don Quixote's armor transport us to a world of chivalry and delusion. Rowling's quick strokes capture the essence of a character's appearance, allowing readers to fill in the blanks with their own imagination. It's about knowing when to zoom in on the texture of a fabric and when to zoom out to capture the grandeur of a landscape.

Walking the Scene - Creating a Tangible Stage

Imagine stepping into a scene and exploring it like a tourist in a foreign city. That's the power of a tangible stage. Authors guide us through spaces with the precision of tour guides, allowing us to experience the environment as if we were there.

Whether it's the crowded halls of Hogwarts or the battlefields of Middle-earth, authors show us the nooks and crannies, the intricacies that bring the world to life. They lead us through rooms, down alleyways, and into forests, inviting us to navigate the terrain with their characters. As writers, our job is to make our stages so tangible that readers can feel the cobblestones beneath their feet and the breeze in their hair.

In Conclusion

And there you have it, my fellow visual architects—an exploration of the art of visualizing scenes and settings. From cinematic vision that paints images in the mind to sensory symphonies that engage all the senses, from set dressing that enhances mood to dynamic descriptions that strike the perfect balance, and from tangible stages that allow readers to walk through scenes to the mastery of showing rather than telling.

As we conclude this chapter, let's carry with us the understanding that storytelling isn't just about the grand plot arcs and colorful characters; it's about the tapestry of imagery that we weave. Our words are more than sentences; they're brush strokes that paint worlds, conjuring emotions, sparking imagination, and inviting readers to step into the pages and make them their own.

Chapter 9
Characters' Canvas
Portraits and Progressions

Ahoy, fellow creators of literary personas! We've tilted at windmills, traveled through time, flown among planets, cast spells, and wandered through enchanted realms. Now, let's shift our focus to the vibrant and varied cast of characters that populate these stories—the heroes, the sidekicks, the villains, and everyone in between. Characters aren't just ink on paper; they're living, breathing souls that guide us through the narrative. So, arm yourselves with pens and parchment, and let's paint the portraits and progressions of characters that leap from the pages.

Character Arcs - From Flawed to Fulfilled

Every character is a canvas waiting to be painted with growth, transformation, and fulfillment. The art of crafting character arcs is about taking flawed individuals and shaping them into heroes we root for. Whether it's Don Quixote's delusions turning into self-awareness or Harry Potter's journey from a boy to a leader, character arcs are the emotional core of a story.

These arcs follow a trajectory—from the initial state to a point of transformation and, ultimately, fulfillment. It's the journey from fear to courage, from ignorance to wisdom, and from doubt to self-belief. A character's arc mirrors our own journey through life's challenges and triumphs, making them relatable and endearing.

Dialogue Dynamics - Speaking Beyond Words

"Words are, in my not so humble opinion, our most inexhaustible source of magic." Albus Dumbledore's words ring true not just in the wizarding world, but in storytelling itself. Dialogue isn't just about characters talking; it's about revealing their thoughts, emotions, and relationships. It's a dance of words that conveys more than the spoken lines.

Think of Don Quixote's humorous conversations with Sancho Panza or the heart-to-heart talks between Harry and his friends. Dialogue dynamics involve the unsaid—the subtext beneath the spoken words. It's the hidden motives, the unspoken desires, and the conflicts bubbling beneath the surface. Crafting dialogue is like choreographing a ballet of emotions and intentions.

Sidekicks and Foils - Supporting the Main Cast

Heroes shine brighter in the company of sidekicks and foils—characters that provide contrast, balance, and depth. Sancho Panza's earthy wisdom complements Don Quixote's delusions, while Samwise Gamgee's loyalty and humility enhance Frodo's journey in Middle-earth.

Sidekicks aren't just comedic relief; they're essential to the protagonist's growth. They challenge, support, and provide perspective. Foils, on the other hand, are the antagonist's counterpart—the mirror that reflects their flaws and motivations. Whether they're providing comic relief or echoing the deeper themes of the narrative, sidekicks and foils are the characters that elevate the main cast.

Villains with Depth - The Antagonist's Journey

No hero shines without a worthy adversary. Villains aren't just evil for the sake of it; they're complex characters with motivations, desires, and backgrounds. From the enigmatic Dark Lord Voldemort to the calculating Miss Havisham, antagonists are as multi-dimensional as the protagonists they oppose.

Villains' journeys often parallel the heroes'. They, too, face challenges and make choices that shape their path. Exploring their motivations and backstory adds depth to the narrative. A well-crafted antagonist challenges the hero not just physically, but morally and emotionally, forcing them to confront their own weaknesses.

Relationships We Love
Building Dynamic Bonds

Dynamic relationships breathe life into stories. Think of Don Quixote's eccentric interactions with the people he meets, the steadfast friendships in the wizarding world, and the mentorship between Gandalf and Frodo. Relationships aren't just filler; they're the heart of human connection.

Writers create bonds that resonate with readers because they reflect the complexities of real relationships. From mentor-mentee dynamics to camaraderie among friends, these relationships showcase loyalty, betrayal, growth, and the power of love. It's the banter between characters, the shared history, and the conflicts that make relationships feel authentic.

In Conclusion

And there you have it, my fellow creators of characters—a deep dive into the craft of painting portraits and progressions. From character arcs that mirror personal growth to dialogue dynamics that reveal hidden truths, from sidekicks and foils that enrich the main cast to villains with depth that challenge the hero, and from relationships that breathe life into the narrative to the tapestry of personalities that populate our tales.

As we conclude this chapter, let's carry with us the understanding that characters aren't just creations; they're mirrors that reflect the human experience. They're the lenses through which we view the world of the story, the anchors that ground us in its reality. So, as you embark on your own writing endeavors, remember that characters aren't just ink on paper; they're the lifeblood of your narrative. Onward, to the final chapter where we distill these insights into writing tips that will guide your own literary odysseys!

Chapter 10
Plot Weaving
Strategies for Engaging Plots

Greetings, fellow weavers of narrative tapestries! We've charged at windmills, wandered through cities, explored fantastical realms, soared among stars, and ventured through magical academies. But what keeps us turning pages and our hearts racing? The plot—the intricate web that hooks readers, pulls them along a journey, and leaves them breathless at the final words. So, grab your quills and inkpots, for we're diving into the art of plot weaving—the secret ingredient that turns a collection of words into a gripping story.

The First Hook
Capturing Attention from the Start

Picture this: "In a hole in the ground, there lived a hobbit." Ah, those opening lines of "The Hobbit"! A well-crafted first hook is the reader's ticket into the story's world. Whether it's Don Quixote charging into imagined battles or Harry Potter receiving a letter from Hogwarts, the first hook is the lighthouse that guides readers into the narrative storm.

A strong hook isn't just about action; it's about intrigue. It's about planting questions that demand answers. Why does Don Quixote mistake windmills for giants? What's special about Harry's scar? The first hook is the promise of adventure, and the reader's curiosity is the wind that fills the sails.

Rising and Falling
Mastering the Tides of Tension

Plot is a symphony of tension and release, a roller coaster of emotions that keeps readers invested. From the initial conflict to the climax and resolution, the rise and fall of tension is what propels the story forward. It's the anticipation of what's around the corner and the satisfaction of seeing it revealed.

Tension isn't just about physical danger; it's about stakes that matter. It's the emotional turmoil of Sydney Carton's sacrifice, the ethical dilemmas of Frodo's journey, and the mystery of the Philosopher's Stone. Plotting is about knowing when to tighten the tension and when to give readers a breather—a rhythm that mimics the heart's beat.

Plot Twists Unveiled
Crafting Surprises with Purpose

Ah, the plot twist—a curveball that sends readers reeling. But a plot twist isn't a magician's trick; it's a tool that reshapes the narrative landscape. Whether it's the revelation of Quixote's delusions or the unexpected friendship in "The Little Prince," a well-crafted twist is like a puzzle piece that snaps the narrative into a new configuration.

A plot twist isn't a gimmick; it's a revelation that adds depth. It's about planting breadcrumbs of foreshadowing and watching readers connect the dots. A twist can be a hidden motivation, a change of allegiance, or a surprising connection. It's the element of surprise that keeps readers engaged and invested in uncovering the truth.

Subplots with Impact
Enriching the Story Experience

Subplots are like spice in a dish—they add layers of flavor and complexity. Think of the parallel stories in "A Tale of Two Cities" or the unfolding mysteries of "Harry Potter." Subplots aren't distractions; they're the threads that interweave with the main narrative, enriching the story experience.

Subplots can serve various purposes—they can provide context, add depth to characters, or mirror the main conflict. They can be romantic subplots, side quests, or moral dilemmas that characters face. Just like in real life, subplots give the story texture, creating a sense of a world that's larger than the protagonist's journey.

Resolutions that Resonate
Satisfying the Reader

The final chords of a symphony are just as important as the opening notes. A satisfying resolution ties up loose ends, answers lingering questions, and leaves readers with a sense of closure. Whether it's Don Quixote's realization or the bittersweet farewells in "The Little Prince," the resolution is the destination of the narrative journey.

A good resolution isn't just about wrapping things up; it's about showing how the characters have changed. It's about demonstrating the impact of their journey and the growth they've undergone. Resolutions can be happy or sad, but they should always be earned—reflecting the character's choices and the consequences of their actions.

In Conclusion

And there you have it, my fellow plot weavers—an exploration of the art of crafting engaging plots. From the first hook that captures attention to the rising and falling tension that keeps readers on the edge, from the unveiling of plot twists that surprise and intrigue to the subplots that enrich the story's tapestry, and from the resolutions that provide closure and satisfaction to the symphony of narrative that leaves readers fulfilled.

As we conclude this chapter, let's carry with us the understanding that plot isn't just a sequence of events; it's a journey that takes readers on an emotional roller coaster. It's about planting seeds of curiosity, sprinkling surprises, and crafting a satisfying destination. So, as you embark on your own writing endeavors, remember that your plot is the vessel that carries readers through your narrative seas. Onward, to the final chapter where we distill these insights into writing tips that will illuminate your path to storytelling greatness!

Chapter 11
Building Worlds
Creating Immersive Settings

Ahoy, architects of alternate realities! We've journeyed through windmills, cities, magical realms, planets, and even the corridors of Hogwarts. But what makes these worlds feel as real as our own? It's the art of world-building—the craft of creating immersive settings that readers can step into and explore with wonder. So, gather 'round as we unravel the mysteries of crafting worlds that resonate, intrigue, and transport readers to new horizons.

World-Building Essentials
Rules and Exceptions

Every world comes with its own rules, its own physics, and its own logic. Whether it's the tilted reality of Don Quixote's chivalrous delusions or the intricate magic system of Rowling's wizarding world, world-building is about establishing the groundwork and then artfully sprinkling in exceptions that surprise and intrigue.

Rules give your world structure, and exceptions create surprises. Just as gravity keeps us grounded on Earth, exceptions like a talking cat in a world of non-talking animals add whimsy and intrigue. A well-built world isn't just a backdrop; it's an ecosystem with its own ecology, politics, and mysteries.

Culture and Customs
Constructing Believable Societies

Culture is the heartbeat of a world. It's the traditions, beliefs, and behaviors that shape characters' lives. From the etiquette of "A Tale of Two Cities" to the wizarding customs of "Harry Potter," cultures give depth and context to characters' actions.

Building cultures isn't just about inventing quirky traditions; it's about understanding the why behind them. Just as real-world cultures are shaped by history, environment, and social dynamics, fictional cultures should reflect these influences. It's about creating societies that feel both familiar and alien—a reflection of the human experience in fantastical settings.

Geography Matters
Mapping Landscapes and Beyond

Geography isn't just about pretty landscapes; it's about shaping characters' journeys and interactions. From the rolling hills of the Shire to the treacherous paths of Mordor, geography isn't just a backdrop; it's a living entity that guides the narrative.

Map-making isn't just for fantasy novels; it's a tool that helps you understand the layout of your world. How does the terrain affect trade routes, communication, and power dynamics? Whether it's a sweeping fantasy realm or a city block, geography influences the story's trajectory and the characters' choices.

Magic Systems and Rules
Establishing Internal Logic

Ah, magic—the element that adds wonder and mystery to worlds. But magic isn't a free pass to do anything; it needs rules and limitations to make it believable. Think of Tolkien's intricate language-based magic or Rowling's spellcasting system with its incantations and wand movements.

Magic systems should have internal logic. What are the costs of using magic? What are its limitations? How does it shape the world's history and culture? A well-defined magic system adds depth and intrigue, while an overly powerful one can undermine tension. Magic should be a tool that characters use, but it shouldn't be the solution to all their problems.

The World as a Character
Infusing Life into Environments

In the greatest stories, the world isn't just a backdrop; it's a character that shapes events and influences characters. Think of how Middle-earth's changing landscapes mirror the characters' emotional journeys or how Hogwarts itself becomes a haven and a challenge for Harry.

Infusing life into environments means making them dynamic. Just as characters evolve, so should the world. Seasons change, cities rise and fall, and landscapes transform. The world reacts to characters' actions, just as characters react to the world's challenges. As writers, our worlds should be as alive and breathing as the characters themselves.

In Conclusion

And there you have it, my fellow world-builders — an exploration of the art of creating immersive settings. From establishing rules and exceptions that give your world structure to constructing believable cultures and customs, from mapping landscapes that guide characters' journeys to crafting magic systems with internal logic, and from treating the world as a character that evolves to adding depth through geography.

As we conclude this chapter, let's carry with us the understanding that world-building isn't just about describing landscapes; it's about shaping the very fabric of the narrative. Our worlds are the stages upon which our characters dance, the backdrops that elevate their stories, and the immersive playgrounds that readers step into. So, as you embark on your own writing journeys, remember that the worlds you build are as rich and complex as the characters that inhabit them. Onward, to the final chapter where we distill these insights into writing tips that will guide your pen toward storytelling brilliance!

Chapter 12
Words That Work
Writing Tips from the Greats

Hello, fellow scribblers and scribes! We've embarked on a grand adventure through windmills, cities, enchanted lands, stars, and the hallowed halls of Hogwarts. Now, it's time to gather around the virtual campfire and listen to the sage advice of the literary greats—those ink-stained pioneers who've paved the way for us to pen our own tales of wonder. Let's dive into a treasure trove of writing wisdom that will infuse your storytelling with brilliance and breathe life into your narratives.

Lessons from Literary Legends
Wisdom from Classic Authors

Classic authors are like the wise elders of the literary realm, beckoning us to sit at their feet and soak in their teachings. From Cervantes to Dickens, Tolkien to Saint-Exupéry, and Rowling to the rest, their works are our textbooks, and their words are our mantras.

These literary legends teach us the power of themes that resonate across generations, the magic of crafting characters that feel alive, and the art of intertwining plot and meaning. They remind us that storytelling is more than entertainment; it's a way to explore the human experience, to confront the complexities of life, and to leave a lasting impact.

Embracing Originality
Finding Your Unique Voice

In a world of literary echoes, it's your voice that sets you apart. From Don Quixote's delusional gallantry to the Little Prince's allegorical charm, every author's voice is a fingerprint—a mark of individuality on the canvas of literature.

Embrace your quirks, your idiosyncrasies, and your passions. Your unique perspective is your greatest asset. Just as Sancho Panza is Don Quixote's loyal companion, your voice will guide readers through your narrative adventures. Originality isn't just a badge of honor; it's a superpower that breathes life into your words.

Reading like a Writer
Learning from Bestsellers

Imagine reading as if every page were a classroom, every sentence a lesson, and every plot twist a revelation. Reading like a writer isn't passive; it's an active exploration of technique, style, and structure. From "A Tale of Two Cities" to "Harry Potter," every bestseller is a treasure trove of insights.

Examine how Dickens masterfully blends historical events with personal stories, how Rowling expertly plants clues and surprises, and how Tolkien's world-building resonates like a symphony. Dissect their dialogues, analyze their pacing, and unravel their character arcs. When you read with writerly eyes, the books on your shelf become mentors and guides.

Critique and Growth
Refining Your Writing through Feedback

Just as Don Quixote learns from his mistakes and adapts his tactics, so should we writers. Constructive feedback is our armor and shield—it guards us from blind spots and fuels our growth. Seek out fellow writers, beta readers, and mentors who can offer insights that elevate your craft.

But remember, not all feedback is golden. Just as Quixote's worldview is skewed by his delusions, feedback can be colored by personal tastes. Learn to sift through critiques, identifying patterns and areas for improvement. Embrace criticism with humility and gratitude, for it's the whetstone that sharpens your narrative sword.

Perseverance and Passion
Nurturing Your Writer's Journey

Writing is a journey, much like Don Quixote's quest for knighthood. There are obstacles, setbacks, and moments of doubt. But just as Quixote charges on despite adversity, so must we persevere. Passion is our trusty steed; it carries us through the long stretches and guides us through the fog of uncertainty.

Embrace the joy of creation, the thrill of discovery, and the satisfaction of crafting sentences that sing. Be prepared for the windmills of self-doubt and the giants of writer's block, but remember that passion is your compass. As long as your heart beats with the rhythm of storytelling, you'll continue to conquer literary landscapes.

In Conclusion

And there you have it, dear writers—a collection of writing tips from the greats, presented with the wit and wisdom that have guided us through this literary odyssey. From the lessons of classic authors to the embrace of originality, from reading like a writer to refining your craft through feedback, and from perseverance fueled by passion to the unwavering commitment to your writer's journey.

As we conclude this chapter, let's carry with us the understanding that writing isn't just about putting words on paper; it's about joining the grand tradition of storytelling. We're not just crafting narratives; we're shaping worlds, sharing emotions, and connecting with readers across time and space. So, as you embark on your own literary quests, remember that your words have the power to touch hearts, inspire minds, and create magic. Onward, dear writers, to the realms of creativity and the boundless horizons of imagination!

Chapter 13
From Concept to Creation
Nurturing Your Novel

Greetings, my fellow creators of literary galaxies! We've explored windmills, traversed cities, embraced magic, and learned from the greats. Now, it's time to delve into the heart of writing—transforming that spark of inspiration into a full-fledged novel that bursts with life. Grab your pens, your coffee mugs, and your inner muse, as we embark on the journey from concept to creation, navigating the rough seas of writerly challenges and basking in the golden rays of artistic accomplishment.

Sparking Inspiration
Finding Ideas that Ignite

Ah, the elusive muse! It's that lightning bolt of inspiration that strikes when you least expect it. Whether it's the whimsicality of "The Little Prince" or the magic of "Harry Potter," inspiration is the nucleus of your creation.

Ideas are everywhere—whispering in the wind, hidden in dreams, and nestled in the mundane. Eavesdrop on conversations, explore unusual corners of the internet, or let your mind wander through history. Remember, inspiration isn't a one-time affair; it's a lifelong fling with creativity. Embrace the mundane and turn it into magic, for inspiration thrives in the ordinary.

Outlining vs. Discovery
Planning Your Writing Journey

To outline or not to outline, that is the question! Some writers swear by meticulous outlines, while others let the narrative flow like a river. Whether you're a meticulous architect like Tolkien or an explorer like Cervantes, the path you choose is uniquely yours.

Outlining offers structure, a roadmap for your journey. It's the blueprint that helps you stay on track and avoid meandering. Discovery, on the other hand, is about chasing your characters down rabbit holes, letting the narrative evolve organically. Find the balance that works for you, and remember that the journey is just as important as the destination.

Overcoming the Blank Page
Techniques to Start Writing

Ah, the blank page—the vast expanse that taunts writers and dares them to conquer it. But fear not, for there are tools to banish the white void. The secret? Start writing, even if it's nonsense. The first draft is about pouring thoughts onto the page, like Don Quixote charging at windmills.

Try timed writing sessions, where you scribble furiously for a set period. Or write the most ridiculous sentence you can think of—anything to break the ice. Remember, you can't edit a blank page, so let your words flow like a river. The goal is to capture your thoughts, to bridge the gap between your mind and the page.

First Drafts Unleashed
Embracing Imperfection

First drafts are the wild horses of the writing world—untamed, unpredictable, and often messy. But remember, even Don Quixote stumbled before he charged ahead. First drafts aren't meant to be perfect; they're meant to be written.

Give yourself permission to write terribly. Allow characters to contradict themselves and let plot holes yawn like chasms. It's all part of the process. The key is to keep going, to cross the finish line. You're building the skeleton of your story, and later drafts will be the flesh and blood that bring it to life.

Revising with Purpose
Polishing Your Masterpiece

Once you've spilled your thoughts onto the page, it's time to sculpt your masterpiece. Much like refining a knight's armor, revising is about perfecting the details. Just as Dickens honed his prose and Tolkien crafted his languages, revision is where your story truly takes shape.

Step back, let your draft breathe, and then dive in with a critical eye. Look for inconsistencies, refine character motivations, and eliminate excess. Revise for plot coherence, thematic depth, and emotional resonance. Remember, revision isn't just about fixing errors; it's about elevating your story to its true potential.

In Conclusion

And there you have it, dear wordsmiths—a journey through the process of nurturing your novel from a mere spark of inspiration to a polished masterpiece. From sparking ideas that ignite your imagination to choosing between outlining and discovery, from overcoming the blank page's taunts to embracing the glorious imperfection of first drafts, and from revising with purpose to polishing your narrative to a brilliant shine.

As we conclude this chapter, let's carry with us the

understanding that writing is a marathon, not a sprint. It's a voyage of discovery, a process of transformation, and a labor of love. Just as Quixote faced countless challenges on his quest, so will you encounter obstacles and doubts. But remember, every word you write, every revision you make, and every sentence you polish brings you closer to the literary horizon you've set out to conquer. Onward, dear writers, to the realms of creation and the uncharted territories of your storytelling destiny!

Chapter 14
Character Chemistry
Crafting Authentic Relationships

Salutations, architects of interpersonal intrigue! We've explored worlds, traversed time, and embarked on journeys aplenty. But now, it's time to dive into the kaleidoscope of human connections—to unravel the threads that tie characters together and create chemistry that leaps off the page. Prepare to delve into the art of crafting relationships that resonate, enthrall, and mirror the complexities of real-life bonds.

Bonds that Bind
Exploring Different Relationship Dynamics

Characters don't exist in isolation; they're the pieces of a puzzle that fit together to create a narrative mosaic. From the kinship between Don Quixote and Sancho Panza to the fellowship of the "Lord of the Rings," relationship dynamics are the mortar that holds the story's bricks together.

Consider mentor-mentee relationships, sibling rivalries, or the silent camaraderie of battle-hardened comrades. Whether it's harmony or tension, the dynamics between characters shape the narrative's rhythm. Unearth their shared history, their opposing values, and the hidden conflicts that simmer beneath the surface.

Love and Beyond
Navigating Romantic Elements

Ah, romance—the dance of hearts, the flutter of butterflies, and the chemistry that lights up the page. From Elizabeth Bennet and Mr. Darcy to the star-crossed lovers of "Romeo and Juliet," romantic relationships are a magnet for readers' emotions.

But crafting compelling romances isn't just about writing lovey-dovey scenes; it's about creating characters who complement and challenge each other. Explore their individual desires, fears, and quirks, and let those traits fuel their chemistry. Remember, romance isn't only about love; it's about growth, compromise, and the journey of two souls intertwining.

Friends and Foes
Developing Compelling Connections

It's not just romantic relationships that make the narrative world go 'round; friendships and rivalries are equally vital. Think of the camaraderie between Harry, Ron, and Hermione, or the enmity that fuels the antagonists of "A Tale of Two Cities."

Friends provide support, challenges, and comic relief. Rivals add tension, competition, and layers to characters' motivations. These connections aren't just add-ons; they're windows into characters' souls. Delve into the origins of friendships, the reasons behind rivalries, and the moments that test or strengthen these bonds.

Conflict Resolution
Driving the Plot through Interaction

Conflict is the heartbeat of storytelling, and where there's conflict, there's interaction. Consider Quixote's clashes with windmills or the heated confrontations in

"Harry Potter." Character interactions are the sparks that light the fire of the narrative.

Conflict isn't just about throwing characters into turmoil; it's about revealing their true selves. Through dialogue, actions, and reactions, characters clash, negotiate, and evolve. Conflict resolution is a canvas for growth, a medium for revelations, and a driver of the plot's momentum.

Subtext and Chemistry
Hints of Unspoken Emotion

In the realm of relationships, not everything is said out loud. Subtext—the unspoken tension beneath the surface—is where chemistry simmers. Think of the unsaid emotions between characters in "Pride and Prejudice" or the intricacies of unspoken desires in "The Little Prince."

Subtext is a tool of nuance, a wink to the observant reader. It's about showing without telling, implying without stating. It's in the pauses, the lingering glances, and the loaded silences. Subtext is the canvas on which readers paint their own interpretations, creating a sense of intimacy that binds them to the characters.

In Conclusion

And there you have it, dear character conjurers—an exploration of the art of crafting authentic relationships. From the different dynamics that bind characters together to the navigation of romantic elements, from the development of friendships and rivalries to the role of character interaction in driving the plot, and from the subtleties of subtext to the unspoken chemistry that adds depth.

As we conclude this chapter, let's carry with us the understanding that relationships are the heartbeat of human experience, and in the realm of storytelling, they're the veins that pump life into the narrative's body. Whether it's the unbreakable bonds of friendship or the charged currents of romantic tension, relationships are the mirror in which characters see their own reflection, and readers see echoes of their own emotions. Onward, dear writers, to the canvas of connections and the tapestry of emotions that make your stories unforgettable!

Chapter 15
Climactic Heights
Mastering Tension and Resolution

Ahoy, architects of anticipation! We've embarked on quests, unraveled secrets, and witnessed relationships blooming like wildflowers. But now, it's time to scale the literary peaks—the towering climaxes that hold readers captive, the moments of ultimate peril that tie the threads together, and the resolutions that leave us satisfied yet yearning for more. Buckle your belts, dear writers, as we ascend to the climactic heights and unravel the art of tension and resolution that gives stories their ultimate crescendo.

The Point of No Return
Navigating the Climax

Picture this: a windmill tilting knight charging into the unknown, a battle atop Mount Doom, or a lightning-clad wizard facing off against his arch-nemesis. The climax is where tension tightens like a bowstring, where characters' destinies hang in the balance.

But how do you navigate this precarious path? It's all about the stakes. Raise them to heart-pounding levels. Think life and death, love and loss, triumph and tragedy. This is the point of no return, where characters make choices that propel them toward their fates. It's the apex of tension, the heart of the story, and the juncture where everything is at stake.

Showdown Strategies
Crafting Memorable Confrontations

Every great climax comes with a showdown — a dance of wits, a clash of ideals, or a physical battle that leaves readers breathless. From Don Quixote's tilting at windmills to the epic showdowns in "The Lord of the Rings," confrontations are the fireworks that light up the night sky.

Crafting a memorable showdown isn't just about choreographing the fight; it's about revealing character truths. Think of the tension between Frodo's desire to destroy the Ring and Gollum's greed for it. Showdowns are about characters facing their inner demons, confronting their flaws, and making decisions that echo their arcs. It's the culmination of growth, the climax of tension, and the pinnacle of catharsis.

Balancing Act - Resolving Conflicts and Arcs

Once the dust settles and the showdown ends, it's time for the resolutions — the ties that bind loose ends, the arcs that complete, and the conflicts that find closure. From Darnay's self-sacrifice in "A Tale of Two Cities" to the quiet moments of reflection in "The Little Prince," resolutions are the sigh of satisfaction that readers breathe.

Balancing resolutions requires finesse. Tie up major plot threads, but leave room for the characters' journeys to continue off the page. Characters should evolve, but not everything needs to be tied with a neat bow. As you resolve conflicts, consider how they reflect characters' growth and bring their arcs full circle.

The Aftermath
Providing Closure without Tying Up All Ends

After the crescendo comes the aftermath — a time for characters to reflect, heal, and make sense of their new reality. Consider the peace that follows the battles in "The Lord of the Rings" or the bittersweet epilogue of "Harry Potter." The aftermath is about giving closure while leaving a taste of the unknown.

The aftermath isn't about spoon-feeding answers; it's about hinting at possibilities. Characters might experience a mix of triumph and loss, hope and uncertainty. Reflect their emotional states through the narrative's tone and pacing. This is the time for readers to catch their breath, to process the journey, and to imagine the characters' futures.

The Last Line
Leaving a Lasting Impression

Ah, the last line—the parting gift to readers, the lingering echo that reverberates in the mind. Think of the haunting last lines of "A Tale of Two Cities" or the whimsical conclusion of "The Little Prince." The last line is the final brushstroke on the canvas of your narrative.

The last line isn't just an endpoint; it's a springboard. It's the note that lingers, the image that stays, and the emotion that resonates. Whether it's a touch of melancholy, a glimmer of hope, or a twist that leaves jaws agape, the last line should encapsulate the essence of your story and echo in readers' hearts long after they close the book.

In Conclusion

And there you have it, dear architects of anticipation—an expedition to the summits of tension and resolution. From the point of no return that marks the climax to the strategies for crafting memorable showdowns, from the balancing act of resolving conflicts and arcs to the art of providing closure without tying up all ends, and from the aftermath that allows characters to reflect to the lasting impression left by the final line.

As we conclude this chapter, let's carry with us the understanding that tension and resolution are the twin pillars that hold up the grand structure of storytelling. Just as characters navigate their arcs, face their conflicts, and find their resolutions, so too must we writers navigate the peaks and valleys of narrative creation. With tension, we hook readers; with resolution, we satisfy their cravings. So, dear writers, as you ascend the heights of your climactic moments, remember that every step you take shapes the path of emotion that readers will follow, leading them to a denouement that lingers in their minds and hearts. Onward, to the realms of catharsis and the tapestry of narrative conclusion!

Chapter 16
Unforgettable Endings
Closing with Impact

Ahoy, storytellers of the grand finale! We've navigated quests, woven relationships, and mastered climactic heights. But now, we face the ultimate challenge—the art of crafting endings that leave readers spellbound, that reverberate in their minds long after the last page is turned. Buckle up, my fellow narrators, as we embark on the journey to conquer the closing curtain with flair, depth, and lasting impact.

The Art of the Final Image
Leaving Visual Imprints

Close your eyes and picture it—a final image that etches itself into memory, that encapsulates the essence of your tale. Think of the rose in "The Little Prince" or the final sunset in "The Lord of the Rings." The last image is a farewell kiss that lingers.

This isn't just about a pretty picture; it's about symbolism, thematic resonance, and emotional impact. Consider how the final image reflects characters' growth, encapsulates the story's central theme, or leaves a question mark that prompts contemplation. The last image isn't just a bow; it's a ribbon that ties up the narrative's gift.

Resonating Themes
Echoing the Heart of Your Story

Themes are the heartbeat of your narrative, and the ending is where they resound like a final note of a symphony. Whether it's the timeless theme of love in "Pride and Prejudice" or the exploration of identity in "Harry Potter," the ending is where themes find their crescendo.

Revisit your story's core theme and consider how it can be reflected in the resolution. Do characters find redemption, self-discovery, or a new sense of purpose? Themes aren't just pretty words; they're the glue that binds the narrative's elements. Allow them to shine in the closing moments.

Open vs. Closed Endings
Weighing the Possibilities

Ah, the age-old debate—should endings be open like a road ahead or closed like a sealed letter? Both have their merits and pitfalls. Open endings invite readers to ponder possibilities, while closed endings offer satisfaction and closure.

Choose wisely based on your story's tone and themes. If your tale is about exploration and self-discovery, an open ending might spark discussion. If it's a tale of resolution and growth, a closed ending might provide that much-needed sigh of satisfaction. But remember, even open endings should offer a sense of completion, while closed endings can hint at what lies beyond the horizon.

Reader Reflection - Inviting Contemplation

An ending isn't just about tying knots; it's about unraveling thoughts. Consider the reflective closing lines of "Don Quixote" or the bittersweet epilogue of "A Tale of Two Cities." The ending is where readers reflect on the journey.

Invite contemplation by leaving breadcrumbs of meaning. Pose questions that linger, present ambiguities that provoke thought, or offer insights that prompt reevaluation. Just as characters ponder their actions, let readers ponder the story's implications. Give them room to reflect on the characters' journeys and how they mirror the human experience.

Lasting Echoes - Crafting Endings that Linger

The final impression is the lasting one—a footprint in the sands of time that echoes across memory. Think of the haunting conclusions of "The Little Prince" or the philosophical musings in "The Lord of the Rings." The ending is the lingering melody that plays long after the orchestra fades.

Craft an ending that resonates beyond the final page. Think of the emotions you want to leave readers with—wonder, nostalgia, contemplation. Leave a trail of breadcrumbs that guide them back to the story, long after they've closed the book. The last words are the ones that echo in their minds, like the final notes of a haunting melody.

In Conclusion

And there you have it, dear architects of endings—a journey to crafting the unforgettable close. From the art of the final image that leaves visual imprints to resonating themes that echo the story's heart, from the delicate balance of open and closed endings to inviting reader reflection, and from the lasting echoes that craft endings that linger.

As we conclude this chapter, let's carry with us

the understanding that endings are more than just final
punctuation; they're the punctuation marks that leave an
indelible mark on readers' hearts and minds. Whether it's
a whispered question, a poignant image, or a hopeful note,
the ending is the legacy you leave behind. So, dear writers,
as you guide your narrative toward its final destination,
remember that every choice you make shapes the last
impression, the aftertaste, and the resonance that lingers.
Onward, to the realms of finality and the echoes that
resonate through time!

Chapter 17
The Reader's Journey
Creating Immersive Experiences

Greetings, architects of literary worlds and emotional rollercoasters! We've uncovered secrets, navigated climaxes, and journeyed through unforgettable endings. But now, it's time to turn the spotlight onto the other side of the equation—the readers. Yes, you, the master puppeteers of emotions, the conjurers of worlds in their minds. Get ready to explore the delicate dance of empathy, suspense, and pacing that leads readers on an immersive journey they won't soon forget.

Empathy Through Prose
Connecting Readers and Characters

Ah, the magic of fiction—it's not just about words on a page; it's about creating a bridge between characters and readers. Think of how readers feel like they're tilting at windmills alongside Don Quixote or attending classes at Hogwarts in "Harry Potter." Empathy is the thread that weaves this tapestry of connection.

Empathy isn't just about making characters relatable; it's about making them human. Give them flaws, desires, and quirks that mirror the reader's own experiences. Show their vulnerabilities, and readers will see themselves in the characters' struggles. Through empathetic prose, you're handing readers a mirror and a telescope, showing them their reflection while inviting them to peer into another world.

Emotional Rollercoaster
Evoking Genuine Feelings

From heart-pounding excitement to tearful farewells, fiction is a carnival ride of emotions. But here's the secret: it's not just about making readers feel; it's about making them feel genuinely. Think of the emotional highs and lows of "A Tale of Two Cities" or the bittersweet wisdom of "The Little Prince."

To evoke genuine emotions, you must feel them yourself. Immerse yourself in the characters' experiences, channel their emotions, and translate them into words that resonate. Don't manipulate; empathize. If you're moved, chances are your readers will be too. Don't just tug at heartstrings; strum them like a master musician.

Suspense and Satisfaction
Playing with Reader Expectations

Suspense is the spice of literary life, the pinch of unpredictability that keeps readers on the edge. Think of the tension in "The Lord of the Rings" or the mystery of "Harry Potter." But remember, suspense isn't just about throwing in plot twists; it's about playing with reader expectations.

Set up promises and challenges that keep readers guessing. Foreshadow without revealing too much, and deliver twists that make them gasp. Build anticipation like an expert magician, and when the reveal comes, let it be both unexpected and satisfying. Suspense isn't about manipulation; it's about inviting readers to play a guessing game and cheering when they're both right and wrong.

Pacing for Page-Turning
Keeping Readers Engaged

Pacing is the heartbeat of storytelling—the rhythm

that keeps readers flipping pages. Think of the swift pacing of "The Little Prince" or the gradual crescendo in "A Tale of Two Cities." Pacing isn't just about moving fast or slow; it's about orchestration.

Vary your pacing like a skilled conductor. Quicken it during action scenes, allowing short sentences to mimic heartbeats. Slow it down during introspective moments, letting readers savor each thought. Balance tension and release, and remember that pacing isn't just about action; it's about letting readers catch their breath, soak in atmosphere, and stay engaged.

Reading Between the Lines
Allowing Interpretation

Every reader brings their own experiences, beliefs, and imagination to a story. The magic lies in the space between the lines—where their interpretation meets your words. Think of the allegorical layers of "The Little Prince" or the complex themes of "A Tale of Two Cities." Interpretation is a dialogue, a dance of words and readers' minds.

Resist the urge to spell everything out. Leave room for ambiguity, for readers to ponder and question. Plant seeds of thought that they can cultivate in their own minds. Let your narrative be a canvas on which readers paint their own meanings, forging a unique connection that makes your story resonate on a deeply personal level.

In Conclusion

And there you have it, dear maestros of emotional symphonies—an exploration of the reader's journey through empathy, emotional depth, suspense, pacing, and interpretation. From the empathy that connects readers and characters to the emotional rollercoaster that evokes genuine feelings, from the suspense that plays with expectations to pacing that keeps readers engaged, and from the spaces between the lines that allow for interpretation to the dance of minds that turns words into personal meanings.

As we conclude this chapter, let's carry with us the understanding that storytelling is a partnership, a dance between the writer's intention and the reader's interpretation. Just as characters embark on journeys, so too do readers—immersing themselves in your narrative, feeling your words, and letting their minds take flight. So, dear writers, remember that your words are not just vessels of meaning; they're catalysts for imagination, conduits for empathy, and invitations for readers to embark on their own unique journeys through the worlds you create. Onward, to the realm of reader immersion and the tapestry of emotions that makes storytelling an enchanting collaboration!

Chapter 18
Crossing Genres
Blending Styles for Unique Narratives

Greetings, genre-bending maestros! We've journeyed through character chemistry, climactic heights, and the reader's immersive experience. But now, let's step into the realm where genres collide, meld, and morph into something altogether extraordinary. Prepare to dive into the thrilling world of crossing genres, where conventions are challenged, norms are shattered, and narratives transcend labels to create stories that are truly one-of-a-kind.

Genre Mashups
Finding Harmony in Diversity

Ah, the joy of mixing genres—the thrill of adventure in a historical setting, the humor of a fantasy realm, or the intrigue of a mystery within a romance. Genre mashups are the symphonies that play with your reader's expectations and bring unexpected flavors to the narrative feast.

The key is to find harmony within diversity. Seamlessly blend the core elements of each genre, but don't stop there—let them enhance and elevate each other. The result should be a cocktail that leaves readers both pleasantly surprised and deeply satisfied. After all, a genre mashup isn't about throwing ingredients together; it's about crafting a balanced recipe that tantalizes the reader's palate.

Hybrid Heroes
Creating Characters Beyond Stereotypes

Genre-blending isn't just about mixing plot elements; it's also about creating characters that challenge stereotypes and embody the complexity of real life. Think of the multi-dimensional characters in "Don Quixote" or the unexpected heroes of "The Lord of the Rings." Hybrid heroes are the rule-breakers who defy labels.

Consider a swashbuckling scientist or a wizard detective. Break free from the confines of genre expectations and let your characters evolve naturally within the narrative landscape. The key is to ensure that their traits and arcs feel authentic to the world you've crafted. Remember, hybrid heroes aren't just intriguing; they're the characters that stick in readers' minds and inspire them to think beyond the boundaries.

Transcending Labels
Writing Stories with Broad Appeal

Genre-blending isn't about narrowing your audience; it's about expanding it. Think of the universal themes in "A Tale of Two Cities" or the timeless wisdom of "The Little Prince." Transcending labels is the art of weaving a narrative that speaks to readers across genres and generations.

Find the common threads that bind different genres—love, sacrifice, identity, human nature. These are the themes that resonate with us all. Craft a story that draws readers in with a gripping plot but keeps them engaged with themes that touch their hearts. A well-crafted genre-blending narrative is a bridge that connects readers from diverse backgrounds, proving that great storytelling knows no boundaries.

Tropes and Tribulations
Navigating Conventions

Every genre comes with its own set of tropes, conventions, and expectations. Navigating these can be a tricky dance. Think of the way "Harry Potter" introduced magic into a contemporary world or how "The Lord of the Rings" transformed epic fantasy with intricate world-building. Tropes and conventions are like tools; it's how you use them that makes the difference.

Use tropes as building blocks, but don't be afraid to twist and turn them into something fresh. Subvert expectations, challenge norms, and surprise your readers. Tropes can be a playground for innovation, a canvas for your unique voice to shine. Remember, it's not about abandoning conventions; it's about reshaping them to suit your narrative vision.

Genre-Bending Writing
The Power of Innovation

At its heart, genre-bending writing is a dance of innovation—a fusion of creativity, imagination, and fearlessness. It's the magic of weaving mystery into historical fiction, or the wonder of sci-fi elements in a contemporary setting. Genre-bending writing is about pushing boundaries, but it's also about being true to the story you want to tell.

Embrace experimentation, but let it be guided by purpose. Consider the themes, characters, and emotions you want to convey. How can blending genres enhance those elements? How can it elevate the reader's experience? Innovation is about taking risks, but it's also about having a clear vision of where those risks will lead.

In Conclusion

And there you have it, dear genre-bending visionaries—an exploration of the art of blending styles to create narratives that transcend labels and redefine storytelling. From genre mashups that find harmony in diversity to hybrid heroes that challenge stereotypes, from stories that transcend labels to navigating conventions with tropes and tribulations, and from the power of innovation in genre-bending writing.

As we conclude this chapter, let's carry with us the understanding that genre-blending isn't just about mixing and matching; it's about creating something entirely new from the pieces you've chosen. It's about taking the familiar and turning it on its head, surprising and delighting readers with unexpected combinations. So, dear writers, as you navigate the world of genre-bending, remember that you're not just writing a story; you're crafting a unique universe where imagination knows no bounds and creativity reigns supreme. Onward, to the realm where genres collide and new worlds emerge from the collision!

Chapter 19
Writer's Block Busters
Overcoming Creative Hurdles

Greetings, wordsmiths and conquerors of the blank page! We've traveled through lands of characters and climaxes, navigating genres and reader's experiences. But here we stand at the crossroads of every writer's journey—the formidable wall known as writer's block. Fear not, for this chapter is your arsenal of creative weaponry, your guide to shattering the chains of stagnation, and your compass through the stormy seas of uncertainty. Let's journey through the land of writer's block busters and emerge victorious on the other side.

The Myth of the Muse
Cultivating Consistent Creativity

Ah, the elusive muse—the ethereal figure that supposedly bestows inspiration upon the lucky few. But let's unravel the truth: creativity isn't a capricious visitor; it's a skill that can be cultivated. Think of it like a garden that needs tending. The more you nurture it, the more bountiful your harvest.

Cultivating consistent creativity is about creating habits. Set aside dedicated writing time, even if it's just a few minutes each day. Train your brain to associate that time with creativity, and soon, the words will flow more easily. Just as a gardener waters plants daily, nourish your creative mind through regular practice.

Breakthroughs in Blocks
Strategies for Unblocking

Writer's block isn't a boulder that can't be moved; it's a puzzle waiting to be solved. The key is to find the right tool for the job. Experiment with strategies like free writing, changing your environment, or tackling a different section of your project. Think of it as trying different keys until one fits the lock.

Another powerful technique is to write without self-censorship. Embrace the "shitty first draft" philosophy, knowing that you can polish later. Perfectionism is the enemy of progress, but the first draft is the realm of possibility. Write freely, and you might just unearth gems amid the rough.

Prompts and Playfulness
Reigniting Your Imagination

When your creative fire dwindles, it's time to stoke the flames with prompts and playfulness. Think of prompts as sparks that ignite new ideas. They can be as simple as a single word, a random image, or a scenario. Let your imagination run wild without judgment or pressure to produce a masterpiece.

Embrace playfulness like a child exploring a new world. Write a scene in the style of your favorite author, or invent a ridiculous character just for fun. The goal isn't a finished piece, but the joy of creating without the weight of expectations.

Mindfulness and Inspiration
Finding Ideas in Everyday Life

Inspiration isn't a mythical creature that lives in distant lands; it's all around you, waiting to be discovered. Practice mindfulness and observe the world with fresh eyes. Take notes on interesting conversations, intriguing images, or fleeting emotions. Let your daily experiences become the seeds of your stories.

Remember, even mundane moments can be the wellspring of inspiration. The way sunlight filters through trees, the scent of rain, the sound of laughter—these details can infuse your writing with authenticity. So, keep your senses open, and you'll find inspiration in the most unexpected places.

Collaboration and Exploration
Tapping into Collective Creativity

Creativity isn't a solitary endeavor; it's a communal celebration. Engage in collaborations, whether it's co-writing with a fellow wordsmith or brainstorming with friends. Sharing ideas and perspectives can breathe life into your projects and help you overcome hurdles.

Exploration is another gateway to innovation. Dive into new hobbies, read widely, or delve into different art forms. A stroll through an art gallery, a visit to a historical site, or even an afternoon spent experimenting in the kitchen can spark ideas you'd never have encountered otherwise.

Persistence and Patience
Navigating the Ebb and Flow

Here's the truth: even the most prolific writers face obstacles. Writer's block is part of the journey, like stormy weather on a sea voyage. But remember, storms pass. Be persistent, and have patience. The ebb and flow of creativity is a natural rhythm; there will be times of abundance and times of drought.

When you hit a roadblock, don't see it as a dead end; view it as a detour. Keep pushing forward, knowing that the path will clear eventually. Even in the darkest moments of writer's block, your passion for storytelling is the North Star that guides you through.

In Conclusion

And there you have it, dear conquerors of creative hurdles—a comprehensive guide to overcoming writer's block and reigniting your creative spark. From cultivating consistent creativity to breaking through blocks, from using prompts and playfulness to finding inspiration in everyday life, and from embracing collaboration and exploration to navigating the ebb and flow of persistence and patience.

As we conclude this chapter, let's carry with us the understanding that writer's block is not an insurmountable barrier; it's a challenge that can be conquered with the right tools and mindset. Just as characters face obstacles in their journeys, so too do writers face obstacles in their creative endeavors. But like any hero, you have the power to rise above and continue the quest for the perfect story. So, dear writers, as you confront writer's block head-on, remember that the pen is mightier than the block, and your imagination is your most potent weapon. Onward, to the realm of creativity unbound and stories waiting to be told!

Chapter 20
Crafting Your Bestseller
Lessons from the Classics

Ahoy, aspiring bestseller architects! We've embarked on a journey through windmills, cities, rings, and beyond, uncovering the secrets of crafting compelling narratives. But now, as we stand at the threshold of this final chapter, it's time to distill the wisdom gleaned from our literary exploration. Prepare to arm yourself with the lessons of the classics as we delve into the art of crafting your very own bestseller. Buckle up, for we're about to embark on the grand finale!

Literary Alchemy
Combining Elements for Success

Creating a bestseller is like mixing the perfect potion—a dash of character development, a sprinkle of world-building, a dollop of plot twists. Just as alchemists sought the philosopher's stone, writers seek the magical formula for storytelling success.

The key is to blend elements harmoniously. Characters should drive the plot, while the plot should reveal their depths. World-building should be immersive, but not overwhelming. Tension should rise, and resolutions should resonate. In the end, it's not just about one ingredient; it's about creating a symphony where every note contributes to the crescendo.

Start Strong, Finish Stronger
Applying Lessons from Endings

The opening lines are a welcoming handshake, but the ending is a lasting embrace. Think of the enigmatic opening of "Don Quixote" and the poignant closing of "The Little Prince." Your book's beginning hooks, but its ending haunts.

Apply lessons from classic endings. The final chapter should echo the themes, bring character arcs to completion, and leave readers with a lingering question or thought. Think of it as the period at the end of a sentence that invites readers to ponder. Start strong to capture attention, but finish stronger to leave a mark.

Characterization Mastery
Bringing Depth to Your Cast

Characters are more than ink on paper; they're vessels of emotion, empathy, and growth. Think of the complex characters in "A Tale of Two Cities" and the unforgettable fellowship in "The Lord of the Rings." Characterization is the soul that breathes life into your narrative.

Mastery lies in depth, not just complexity. Give characters flaws and virtues, aspirations and fears. Show their quirks and vulnerabilities. Let them make mistakes, and let them evolve through their experiences. Characters are the heart of your story, and their journey is the pulse that keeps readers engaged.

Plot Perfection
Constructing Stories that Keep Readers Hooked

A plot isn't just a sequence of events; it's a tapestry of tension and release. Think of the intertwining narratives in "A Tale of Two Cities" and the epic journey in "The

Lord of the Rings." Plot perfection is the rollercoaster that keeps readers gripping the edge of their seats.

Create a plot that's a delicate dance of anticipation and surprise. Introduce conflict, raise stakes, and provide moments of catharsis. Weave subplots that enrich the narrative tapestry and mirror character growth. Make every event matter; let each chapter leave readers yearning for more. Your plot should be an intricate puzzle, its pieces fitting together to reveal a stunning picture.

Building Worlds, Forging Legends
Balancing World-Building and Plot

World-building is the forge where the sword of your plot is tempered. Think of the immersive worlds in "The Lord of the Rings" and the whimsical planets in "The Little Prince." World-building is the backdrop that turns a story into a legend.

Balance is the key to successful world-building. Develop the setting enough to immerse readers, but don't let it overwhelm the plot. Every detail should serve a purpose, whether it's advancing the story, reflecting themes, or enhancing character development. Remember, the world isn't just a stage; it's a character in its own right.

In Conclusion

And there you have it, dear architects of bestsellers—the culmination of our journey through classic narratives and the lessons they impart. From the art of literary alchemy that combines elements for success to applying lessons from endings that linger, from characterization mastery that brings depth to your cast to plot perfection that keeps readers hooked, and from building worlds that forge legends to the delicate balance between world-building and plot.

As we conclude this chapter and this book, let's carry with us the understanding that crafting a bestseller is a grand symphony of words, a dance of characters and plot, and a tapestry woven with themes and emotions. Just as the classics have illuminated our path, now it's your turn to tread that path and create stories that resonate with generations. So, dear writers, as you embark on your own literary adventures, remember that your voice is unique, your perspective is invaluable, and your stories have the power to touch hearts and minds. Onward, to the realm of bestsellers waiting to be written and readers eager to be enchanted!

Appendix
Writing Exercises and Prompts

Congratulations, intrepid adventurers of the written word! As we conclude this literary odyssey, it's time to equip you with a treasure chest of writing exercises and prompts that'll keep your creativity ablaze and your skills sharp. Consider this your toolbox, your playground, and your secret chamber of inspiration. Dive in, experiment, and let your imagination soar to new heights.

Character Building
Unveiling Multidimensional Protagonists

Characters are the heart of any story, so why not give them the spotlight they deserve? Start by crafting a character profile—a detailed dossier that includes their physical traits, personality quirks, fears, dreams, and backstory. But let's add a twist: assign your character an unexpected trait or secret that challenges their archetype. How does a fearless knight secretly have a fear of horses? What if the sweet librarian is also an amateur cage fighter?

Setting Sketches
Breathing Life into Your Story's World

A vivid setting can transform your story from a mere stage to a living, breathing universe. Choose a location, whether it's a cozy café, a futuristic city, or a mystical forest. Now, describe it from three different perspectives: the eyes of a child, the eyes of a tourist, and the eyes of someone who's lived there for decades. How does each perspective reveal new layers of the setting's essence?

Plotting Practice
Crafting Intriguing Story Arcs

Plotting is like orchestrating a symphony of events. Take a classic tale you love and twist it by changing the setting, time period, or genre. What would "Romeo and Juliet" look like in a cyberpunk dystopia? How about "Alice in Wonderland" set during the American Revolution? Play with these elements, and watch new narratives unfold before your eyes.

Dialogue Dexterity
Creating Authentic Conversations

Dialogue isn't just words exchanged; it's the rhythm of your characters' voices. Choose two characters who couldn't be more different—an alien and a cowboy, a ghost and a tech mogul, a pirate and a librarian. Write a conversation between them, focusing on how their distinct personalities shape their words. Can they find common ground despite their differences?

Climactic Moments
Building Tension and Resolution

Climactic moments are the beating heart of your story. Choose a mundane situation—a family dinner, a walk in the park, a job interview—and inject it with tension. What if a disagreement erupts at the family dinner? What if a sudden storm disrupts the walk? What if the job interview takes an unexpected turn? Craft these moments with escalating tension and a satisfying resolution.

In Conclusion

And there you have it, fellow wordsmiths—an appendix brimming with exercises and prompts to spark your creativity, refine your skills, and push the boundaries of your storytelling. Remember, the path of a writer is one of constant growth, exploration, and curiosity. As you tackle these exercises, let your imagination roam freely, unburdened by expectations. Whether you're crafting multidimensional characters, sketching vibrant settings, plotting thrilling arcs, weaving authentic dialogues, or building climactic moments, you're honing your craft and inching closer to the realm of literary greatness.

So, dear writers, as you venture forth armed with these exercises and prompts, know that every word you write is a step toward realizing your creative potential. Embrace the challenges, cherish the discoveries, and let your stories be your legacy. Onward, to a world of endless creativity and stories that leave a lasting impact!

Acknowledgments
A Literary Gratitude Extravaganza

Ahoy, fellow adventurers in the realm of words! As we close this literary tome, it's time to raise our quills and hearts in a grand symphony of gratitude. What's a journey without companions, after all? So gather 'round, for it's time to give a shout-out to the people and forces that have guided, supported, and fueled the creation of this book. Consider this chapter a virtual bouquet of appreciation, a tapestry woven with heartfelt thanks.

The Muse Whispers
Honoring the Spark of Inspiration

First and foremost, a salute to the elusive muse, the whisperer of ideas, and the igniter of creativity. Whether it's a fleeting thought, a dreamy notion, or an unexpected spark, you, dear muse, are the wellspring from which our stories flow. We raise our quills in gratitude for your unpredictable visits and the magic you bring to our writing lives.

Literary Pioneers
Homage to the Classics

To the timeless authors who paved the way for storytelling as we know it, we tip our hats and pens. From Cervantes to Dickens, from Tolkien to Saint-Exupéry, and from Rowling to the countless others who have gifted us with worlds to explore and characters to embrace—your legacies continue to light our literary paths. We thank you for the wisdom you've shared through your masterpieces.

Writing Companions
Friends, Family, and Fellow Writers

To the friends and family who've endured our writerly quirks, listened to our plot musings, and provided much-needed encouragement—your support has been the wind beneath our wings. And to our fellow writers, our partners-in-crime in this journey, you've been our sounding boards, our sources of inspiration, and our solace in the face of writer's block. Let's raise a virtual toast to our shared passion and camaraderie.

Teachers and Mentors
Guiding Lights of Wisdom

To the teachers and mentors who've bestowed upon us the gift of knowledge and guided us through the labyrinth of literary craft—your wisdom has been the compass steering us in the right direction. Whether it's lessons in grammar, insights into character psychology, or the delicate art of crafting dialogue, your influence lives on in our pages.

Readers and Explorers
The Heartbeat of Every Tale

A round of applause for the readers, the ones who embark on the adventures we've penned. You, dear readers, are the ones who breathe life into our stories, who experience the highs and lows, the laughter and tears, and who take our words into your hearts. You complete the circle of storytelling, and for that, we are eternally grateful.

In Conclusion

As we bid adieu to this literary journey, let's take a moment to reflect on the tapestry of connections, influences, and gratitude that weaves itself through our lives as writers. From the inspiration of the muse to the legacy of classic authors, from the support of friends and family to the guidance of mentors, from the camaraderie of fellow writers to the embrace of readers—the journey is richer for the presence of each and every one.

So, dear companions on this literary voyage, as you close the final pages of this book, remember that every writer stands on the shoulders of giants, and every story is a symphony of voices, past and present. With hearts full of appreciation, let us carry forward the torch of storytelling, with the hope that our words will touch lives, ignite imaginations, and leave a mark on the tapestry of literature. Onward, to new stories, new horizons, and new journeys yet to be penned!